T0161345

THE GRIFFIN POETRY PRIZE
Anthology 2017

Published in Canada in 2017 and in the USA in 2017 by House of Anansi Press Inc.
www.houseofanansi.com

21 20 19 18 17   1 2 3 4 5

Library and Archives Canada Cataloguing in Publication

Cataloguing data available from Library and Archives Canada

Cover design: Chloé Griffin and Kyra Griffin
Cover image: Chloé Griffin
Inside cover image: *Palmtrees* by Simone Gilges
Typesetting: Laura Brady

We acknowledge for their financial support of our publishing program the Canada Council for the Arts, the Ontario Arts Council, and the Government of Canada through the Canada Book Fund.

Printed and bound in Canada

THE GRIFFIN POETRY PRIZE

Anthology 2017

A SELECTION OF THE SHORTLIST

Edited by SUE GOYETTE

ANANSI

CONTENTS

CANADIAN SHORTLIST

PREFACE

In the last few months, I received six hundred and seventeen invitations to quiet my noise, tune my listening fork, and embark into a new ecosystem of idea and language, of weather system and atmosphere. Each book a request to begin reading with an openness that would become its own discipline.

I mostly read the books in a house in the woods with no Internet, a wood stove, and some magnificent pine trees. The lake was either skidding or smoothing itself; a couple of hares would come close enough for me to marvel at their ears, translucent pink maps of veins, and how vitally alert they were. I met a frog that moved vertically, doing a kind of cha-cha between rocks that was beguiling and unexpected. One day I disrupted five herons that took to the sky panicked, putting expanse into a long-winged perspective. All of these things contributed to the collective fluency of the landscape. It kept me grounded and instructed me somehow. That helped assuage my feelings of being out to sea. This fluency seemed kin to the natural cohesiveness, the vitality good work has that I used like a compass. Stacks of over six hundred books of poems are potent and can be overwhelming company. I needed a reliable sense of direction.

A ten-minute drive from this house is a diner where they've lucked upon the idea of deep-frying baby potatoes whole, which taste even better than they sound. In the diner, there's a photo of one of the last lighthouse keepers in the community. His face had traded something with the ocean. His eyes knew horizon and rock as intimately as we know our beds. The man was weathered and intent-looking. I'd try to sit at the table under him for how his look helped with the reading. The same way I keep a photo of Lorca on my desk. Both their gazes hold that which refuses to be snared into words but is vital to poetry. Lorca would call it the duende. And what would our lighthouse keeper say? Something that would get us back to land but not before we had tasted humility and learned to know arriving at a rocky shore as a good enough fortune. The last lighthouse keeper in Port Mouton helped my reading as well.

The six hundred plus books began to arrive before and continued arriving after the American presidential election. As we all know, the outcome of that election changed the world, darkened and intensified it. Something deplorable was happening every day. What I didn't expect was how it also changed my relationship to the piles of those books. Before the election, they were poetry collections that were singular in their reach. After the election, each book represented the person who was taking the time to do the work of art, bent and attending to their words and following the trail those words were leaving. This is no small thing. It is a practice that seems even more important, more crucial now. It shares the fortitude of protest that defies commodity and "fake news" and can rekindle our curiosity, our imaginative thinking to help move us forward with a realigned spirit. The good feeling I garnered from their collective and cohesive camaraderie endures in me still.

The pre-eminent company of my fellow jurors, Joan Naviyuk Kane and George Szirtes, endures as well. If each poetry collection is an ecosystem, Joan and George helped me navigate books whose lay of the land I missed somehow. Our task was to choose seven collections we agreed were exceptionally engaged and unexpected. Each of us, I'm sure, has our own private sorrows, books we brought with us into those conversations that didn't make it to our final lists. Reconciling these losses is one of the difficulties of adjudicating art. Far easier is feeling grateful to The Griffin Trust for Excellence in Poetry. And grateful for the work it does in maintaining and contributing to the vitality of our poetry community, and also for the proficient Ruth Smith, who corralled our time and kept us on track. Easier still is this: a celebration of these seven fine poets and the vital work they've given us.

Sue Goyette, April 2017

THE GRIFFIN POETRY PRIZE
Anthology 2017

INTERNATIONAL
SHORTLIST

JANE MEAD

World of Made and Unmade

Jane Mead's poem *World of Made and Unmade* moves with elegance between elegy and harvest, between the work of practical care to the unmooring that loss precipitates. The poem allows for the intrusions of dogs and the laundry room flooding, acknowledging how the force of our days persists in the company of the dying. And how those disruptions are sometimes what can help carry us, sustain us through the experience, realign our spirit, or afford us reprieve. And in the midst of this is the poet's mother, the life she has lived persuasive and just as vital. Mead moves from the days' demands, engaged and articulate, to depict the service, the duty, and the company the dying require. Occasionally, the poem is still, reflective, posited at the bottom edge of the page, engaging in the ongoing conversation and the reckoning. Her language serves loss as a bell serves its chime. In her life, Mead's mother planted and cared for 2001 pecan trees; her legacy, an orchard. In *World of Made and Unmade*, her life asks her daughter's 'How will you spend your courage?' This poem seems that brave response.

. . .
The third time my mother fell
she stopped saying she wanted to die.

*Saying you want to die
is one thing,* she pointed out,
but dying is quite another.

And then she went to bed.

. . .
Outside her window the trees
of her orchard are heavy
with their load of ripening pecans.

The shadow of the Organ Mountains
creeps across the land,
and the blue heron stands on the shore
of the shrunken Rio Grande.

Wichita, Chickasaw, Wichita, Shoshoni:
her every tree, her every row.

—Rincon, NM, July 15

. . .

How will you spend your courage,
her life asks my life.

No courage spent of—
bloodshot/gunshot/taproot/eye.

How will you spend
your courage, how

will you spend your life.

Bloodshot, gunshot, taproot, eye—
and the mind
on its slow push through the world—

. . .
In my dream my mother comes with me.

We are in the meadows we call
The Flats, walking the dogs.

Walk straight past the water trough,
she says, *do not engage the moss.*

Go back to the top of the page,
the dream says, and leave out the suicides.

In my dream I walk and walk.

After a time—no mother.
After a time—no dogs.

Just the field of dry grasses
and me and the walking.

Then just the walking.

. . .

My mother's every exhale is
somewhere between a rasp
and a scream now.

Hospice says they'll bring
phenobarbital in the morning.

Between us we have
—new bottle of morphine
—the dog's phenobarbital
—three syringes of Parry's insulin
—methadone, Haldol, etc.

Parry and I discuss combinations.
We want the best for our mother.

We do not want
to fuck this
one up.

— October 22, +/- 2 a.m.

. . .

On the phone, my brother Whit
says *Don't Google it.*

. . .
Silvia asks whether I ever feel
my mother's presence, the way we do
sometimes with the dead, who can

make themselves felt, who can feel a lot
like the speechless living when they want to,
—as when that great horned owl

stared at me from the deodar tree
while I was thinning radishes—until
I looked up and saw her glaring

and, not knowing what else to do, waved.

Truth is, I do not feel my mother's presence.
Truth is, if ever a person were to fail

to become a disembodied presence it would be

my beautiful and practical mother.

. . .
Her ashes blow off—
grit on the cold wind—
through her orchard, 2001

pecan trees, about which
she wrote me once
from what some considered

her self-exile down
by the Mexican border—
I don't know why

it gives me such pleasure
to cause 2001 living things
to thrive, but it does.

Back then, her new trees stood
just three feet high. She
pruned them standing and carried

her entire harvest around
in a briefcase, looking
for future buyers.

—Rincon, NM, November 19

. . .
In the phone photograph
of us in the orchard now,
Parry holds a tin pitcher

with our mother's ashes
and we three look small,
wizened almost, in our grief.

The trees, formidable
and orderly are losing
their leaves. The pecans

pop out of their casings—
ready for their winter harvest.

Wichita, Chickasaw, Wichita, Shoshoni:
her every tree, her every row.

DONALD NICHOLSON-SMITH

TRANSLATED FROM THE FRENCH WRITTEN BY ABDELLATIF LAÂBI

In Praise of Defeat

In this bilingual book (Laâbi's original French and Nicolson-Smith's English)—a book that is monumental both in size (over 800 pages) and in scope—we meet one of the major poets of our time, one who has lived through great and catastrophic events and responded to them with a passionate, intelligent humanity. Laâbi can move from the simplest short poems about the delights of the body to complex meditations on war, violence, and prison. That he does so in such an open, generous voice (so well communicated by the dedicated translator, since this must have been an epic labour of love for him) is one of the admirable aspects of Laâbi's mind and art. The rhetorical pitch is perfectly judged. There is nothing glib about the eloquence, nor is there anything uncontrolled or self-indulgent about the fury when it rises. The poems are public in the best sense in that they address the reader as an equal, not as from a tower but in the street. The interest in Laâbi's work is intense and growing, and other fine books of translations from his work have become available. But this is a landmark.

Bonjour soleil de mon pays

Bonjour soleil de mon pays
qu'il fait bon vivre aujourd'hui
que de lumière
que de lumière autour de moi
Bonjour terrain vague de ma promenade
tu m'es devenu familier
je t'arpente vivement
et tu me vas comme un soulier élégant
Bonjour pique-bœuf balourd et philosophe
perché là-haut
sur cette muraille qui me cache le monde
te chatouillant les côtes
à petits coups distraits
Bonjour herbe chétive de l'allée
frissonnant en petites rides opalescentes
sous la caresse taquine du vent
Bonjour grand palmier solitaire
planté sur ton échasse grenue
et t'ouvrant comme une splendide tulipe
à la cime
Bonjour soleil de mon pays
marée de présence annihilant l'exil
Que de lumière
que de lumière autour de moi

* * *

J'ai mille raisons de vivre
vaincre la mort quotidienne
le bonheur de t'aimer
marcher au pas de l'espoir

* * *

Good Morning Sun of My Land

Good morning sun of my land
how good it feels to be alive today
so much light
so much light around me
Good morning empty exercise yard
you have become familiar to me
I cross you with a lively step
and you suit me like an elegant shoe
Good morning ponderous and philosophical oxpecker
perched up there
on the wall that hides the world from me
poking at your ribcage
with distracted little movements
Good morning sparse grass in the alley
quivering in opalescent flurries
at the wind's teasing touch
Good morning great lone palm
erect on your cross-grained trunk
blooming at your peak
like a glorious tulip
Good morning sun of my land
tide of presence abolishing exile
So much light
so much light around me

* * *

I have a thousand reasons to live
to vanquish day-to-day death
the joy of loving you
and walking in step with hope

* * *

Tant d'années
à n'avoir jamais connu
la solitude ou l'ennui
tant d'étoiles filantes dans ma tête
La vasque de tendresse murmure
en plein chant
l'étrange bonheur du prisonnier

* * *

La nuit a lâché sa horde de colombes
sur les forêts sensuelles du souvenir
Tu m'apparais
terrifiante de grâces et de promesses
puis c'est le rite
entrecoupé de détonations
de voyeurs hilares puant la cagoule
Je ne suis qu'à moitié homme

* * *

L'eau coule dans ma main
Des gouttelettes irisées
absorbent goulûment le soleil
Rêver n'est que le reflet
de ce presque miracle

* * *

Le sourire éclot de lui-même
Je ne l'arrache pas à ma face
oubliée avec tous les miroirs
Sourire inextinguible
c'est comme ça que je résiste

So many years
without ever knowing
solitude or boredom
so many shooting stars in my head
The reservoir of tenderness hums
in plainsong chant
the prisoner's peculiar happiness

* * *

Night has released its host of doves
into the sensual forests of memory
You appear to me
terrifying with grace and promise
then comes the ritual
punctuated by explosions
from elated voyeurs stinking of the cagoule
I am half a man only

* * *

Water runs onto my hand
Iridescent drops
greedily gobble up the sunshine
Dreaming is merely a reflection
of this near-miracle

* * *

The smile breaks out by itself
I do not wipe it from a face
forgotten along with all mirrors
An inextinguishable smile
my way of resisting

Les camarades dorment
La prison a cessé de tournoyer clans leur tête
Ils naviguent à cœur ouvert
en haute mer de nos passions inédites
Ils sont beaux dans leur sommeil

* * *

C'est encore loin le *temps des cerises*
et des mains chargées d'offrandes immédiates
le ciel ouvert au matin frais des libertés
la joie de dire
et la tristesse heureuse

C'est encore loin le temps des cerises
et des cités émerveillées de silence
à l'aurore fragile de nos amours
la fringale des rencontres
les rêves fous devenus tâches quotidiennes

C'est encore loin le temps des cerises
mais je le sens déjà
qui palpite et lève
tout chaud en germe
dans ma passion du futur

Maison centrale de Kénitra, 1978

* * *

The comrades are asleep
The prison no longer twists and turns their minds
They are sailing with open hearts
on the high seas of our extraordinary passions
They are beautiful as they sleep

* * *

The *temps des cerises* is still far off
along with hands bearing gifts freely offered
a sky open to the new morning of freedoms
the joy of speech
and happy sadness

The cherry season is still far off
with its cities enchanted by silence
the fragile dawn of our loves
the hunger for encounter
the mad dreams become workaday tasks

The cherry season is still far off
but I feel it already
palpitating and quickening
a warm growing embryo
in my passion for the future

Kenitra Prison, 1978

de **L'écorché vif**

Comme les énigmes de l'inquisiteur sont aisées !
Comparons, dit-il, avec celles
que je n'ose parfois me poser à moi-même :

Par quelle tribu occulte es-tu gangrené ?

Es-tu indemne de tout pouvoir ?

As-tu cassé tous les miroirs ?

De quelles infirmités tires-tu ta force ?

Quels sont les tabous de ta droiture ?

Pourquoi ne reconnais-tu que du bout des lèvres l'ampleur de tes
ignorances ?

Ne t'arrive-t-il pas de te contenter de l'à-peu-près de ce que tu aurais
vraiment voulu dire ? D'être irrité par tes plus justes passions ? De
maudire tes superbes raisons de vivre ?

Ne joues-tu pas un peu au martyr ?

from **Skinned Alive**

How easy the inquisitor's questions are!
Compare them, he says, with the questions
I sometimes dare not ask myself:

What hidden tribe gave you gangrene?

Are you utterly untainted by power?

Have you broken all the mirrors?

From what weaknesses do you draw your strength?

What taboos govern your rectitude?

Why do you pay only lip service to the scope of your ignorance?

Do you not sometimes settle for a mere approximation of what you
really wanted to say? Are you not sometimes annoyed by your own
most righteous passions? Do you not sometimes tend to curse your
fine reasons for living?

Are you not a little prone to play the martyr?

Les loups

J'entends les loups
Ils sont bien au chaud dans leurs maisons de campagne
Ils regardent goulûment la télévision
Pendant des heures, ils comptent à voix haute
les cadavres
et chantent à tue-tête des airs de réclame
Je vois les loups
Ils mangent à treize le gibier du jour
élisent à main levée le Judas de service
Pendant des heures, ils boivent un sang de village
encore jeune, peu fruité
à la robe défaite
le sang d'une terre où sommeillent des charniers
J'entends les loups
Ils éteignent à minuit
et violent légalement leurs femmes

The Wolves

I hear the wolves
They are nice and warm in their country houses
They watch television hungrily
For hours they count the corpses aloud
and sing advertising jingles at the top of their lungs
I see the wolves
Thirteen at table eating the day's kill
electing their Judas of the moment on a show of hands
For hours they drink a local blood
still young, not too fruity
pallid as to color
the blood of a land where mass graves slumber
I hear the wolves
They turn their lights out at midnight
and rape their wives legally

de **Mon cher double**

Mon double
une vieille connaissance
que je fréquente avec modération
C'est un sans-gêne
qui joue de ma timidité
et sait mettre à profit
mes distractions
Il est l'ombre
qui me suit ou me précède
en singeant ma démarche
Il s'immisce jusque dans mes rêves
et parle couramment
la langue de mes démons
Malgré notre grande intimité
il me reste étranger
Je ne le hais ni ne l'aime
car après tout
il est mon double
la preuve par défaut
de mon existence

* * *

from **My Dear Double**

My double
an old acquaintance
whom I visit with moderation
He is a shameless fellow
who plays on my shyness
and has the knack of profiting
from my distractedness
He is the shadow
who follows or precedes me
aping my walk
He even winkles his way into my dreams
and speaks the language of my demons
fluently
Despite our close intimacy
he is still a stranger to me
I neither hate nor love him
for after all
he is my double
the proof by default
of my existence

* * *

ALICE OSWALD

Falling Awake

Alice Oswald's *Falling Awake* presents as a dark text to
(re)turn (in)to, its language of ". . . maybe the last green
places [. . .]" striking bright inscriptions that may have
been "falling for a long time." How fortunate we are to
tread the paths of myth and that which presupposes
it, and us: line, image, lilt. Quite within other declara-
tions, Oswald exalts with great nimbleness: "I notice the
lark has a needle / pulled through its throat." In these
poems, enclosed at times within the old enchantments
of Eurydice, Orpheus, and Tithonus, one wonders about
the problem of being bound to place, to anything at all.
And then, the problem, too, becomes a source of wonder
— albeit tempered by the concise splendour of a mind
that moves quickly within the confines of night and day.
Falling Awake permits the reader to breach lyric time as
the poet explicates the fixed architecture as it flickers by,
"trying over and over its broken line / trying over and over
its broken line."

A Short Story of Falling

It is the story of the falling rain
to turn into a leaf and fall again

it is the secret of a summer shower
to steal the light and hide it in a flower

and every flower a tiny tributary
that from the ground flows green and momentary

is one of water's wishes and this tale
hangs in a seed-head smaller than my thumbnail

if only I a passerby could pass
as clear as water through a plume of grass

to find the sunlight hidden at the tip
turning to seed a kind of lifting rain drip

then I might know like water how to balance
the weight of hope against the light of patience

water which is so raw so earthy-strong
and lurks in cast-iron tanks and leaks along

drawn under gravity towards my tongue
to cool and fill the pipe-work of this song

which is the story of the falling rain
that rises to the light and falls again

Flies

This is the day the flies fall awake mid-sentence
and lie stunned on the window-sill shaking with speeches
only it isn't speech it is trembling sections of puzzlement which
break off suddenly as if the questioner had been shot

this is one of those wordy days
when they drop from their winter quarters in the curtains
      and sizzle as they fall
feeling like old cigarette butts called back to life
blown from the surface of some charred world

and somehow their wings which are little more than flakes
      of dead skin
have carried them to this blackened disembodied question

what dirt shall we visit today?
what dirt shall we re-visit?

they lift their faces to the past and walk about a bit
trying out their broken thought-machines
coming back with their used-up words

there is such a horrible trapped buzzing wherever we fly
it's going to be impossible to think clearly now until next winter
what should we
what dirt should we

Cold Streak

I notice a cold streak
I notice it in the sun
all that dazzling stubbornness
of keeping to its clock

I notice the fatigue of flowers
weighed down by light
I notice the lark has a needle
pulled through its throat

why don't they put down their instruments?
I notice they never pause
I notice the dark sediment of their singing
covers the moors like soot blown under a doorway

almost everything here has cold hands
I notice the wind wears surgical gloves
I notice the keen pale colours of the rain
like a surgeon's assistant

why don't they lift their weight
and see what's flattened underneath it?
I notice the thin meticulous grass,
thrives in this place

Slowed-Down Blackbird

Three people in the snow
getting rid of themselves
        breath by breath

and every six seconds a blackbird

three people in raincoats losing their tracks in the snow
walking as far as the edge and back again
with the trees exhausted
        tapping at the sky

and every six seconds a blackbird

first three then two
passing one eye between them
and the eye is a white eraser rubbing them away

and on the edge a blackbird
trying over and over its broken line
trying over and over its broken line

Sz

good morning to you, first faint breeze of unrest
no louder than the sound of the ear unzipping,
late-comer, mere punctuation between seasons
whom the Chinese call
Sz

forgive me, small-mouth,
I heard you criticise the earth
and stepped outside to see the fields ruffle your cloth,
but you were moving on:
monotonous
vindictive
dust-bearing
scrupulous
one of many mass-produced particles of time
by whom the fruit has small frost-marks
and their hearts are already eroded and I
too

if you think, leaf-thief,
if you think I care
about your soft-spoken
head-in-the-clouds
seizure of another and yet another and yet another hour
then hear me, Sz,
you are so bodiless, so barely there
that I can only see you through starlings
whom you try this way and that like an uncomfortable coat
and then abandon

from Tithonus

    she never quite completes her
sentence but is always almost
    and this is what draws me to the
window too late I notice my head
still balanced on my neck but severed
by light from myself not knowing
but almost

    what a non-sequitur from a seagull
at the height of falling

    as soon as one rook too black goes
into smoky trees saying nothing and
the wood still lost in its inmost
unable
    and mist forms an orderly queue
for the horizon

    green ropes of wind white silks
of field
    and buried under several feet of
colour the eyes can never quite see
out but it is glittering now in the
gaps between things

and the thistle begins to be
properly named and certain of its
spikes
what a chandelier of dock flowers
dangles from the ground inverted
so the morning and I meet up
again but not on talking terms

Music

now a snail the speechless tongue
of one who is introverted and clings
to leaves
pokes out of sleep too feelingly
as if a heart had been tinned and
opened

now laughing mallards pull
themselves together
now swans make straight lines
across water

now webs on twigs now the rapid
whisper of a grasshopper scraping
back and forth as if working at rust

and now a gorse bush as I glance towards
it a sort of swelling yellow-
ness a smelling somehowness
   barely keeps still enough to be
certain
   while a fern unfolds growing
outside the time zone

now   4:32   now   4:33

DENISE RILEY

Say Something Back

The beauty of Denise Riley's book lies in its rejection of the kind of beauty that is ready to hand. In it we meet a mind that scrupulously rejects the grandiose gesture but is not averse to play and tenderness. Or indeed to tragedy. The longest poem in the book, "A Part Song" is about the loss of the poet's son. In it she addresses poetry itself and questions its ability to give appropriate form to such loss. But what might appear to be the bare cupboard of grief is, in her poem, packed with voices, entrances, and movements that doubt their own validity and are, marvellously, all the more valid for that. Beyond the loss there remains the close, firmly disciplined observation of the world, of the humour and pathos at its edges, and the lifelong attempt to allow it its own voice, the willingness, as the book's title has it, to "say something back." Riley's work has always been substantial, but this book is something very special, a full blossoming and gathering.

from **A Part Song**

You principle of song, what are you *for* now
Perking up under any spasmodic light
To trot out your shadowed warblings?

Mince, slight pillar. And sleek down
Your furriness. Slim as a whippy wire
Shall be your hope, and ultraflexible.

Flap thinly, sheet of beaten tin
That won't affectionately plump up
More cushioned and receptive lays.

But little song, don't so instruct yourself
For none are hanging around to hear you.
They have gone bustling or stumbling well away.

What is the first duty of a mother to a child?
At least to keep the wretched thing alive – Band
Of fierce cicadas, stop this shrilling.

My daughter lightly leaves our house.
The thought rears up: *fix in your mind this*
Maybe final glimpse of her. Yes, lightning could.

I make this note of dread, I register it.
Neither my note nor my critique of it
Will save us one iota. I know it. And.

iii

Maybe a retouched photograph or memory,
This beaming one with his striped snake-belt
And eczema scabs, but either way it's framed,
Glassed in, breathed hard on, and curated.
It's odd how boys live so much in their knees.
Then both of us had nothing. You lacked guile
And were transparent, easy, which felt natural.

Each child gets cannibalised by its years.
It was a man who died, and in him died
The large-eyed boy, then the teen peacock
In the unremarked placid self-devouring
That makes up being alive. But all at once
Those natural overlaps got cut, then shuffled
Tight in a block, their layers patted square.

It's late. And it always will be late.
Your small monument's atop its hillock
Set with pennants that slap, slap, over the soil.
Here's a denatured thing, whose one eye rummages
Into the mound, her other eye swivelled straight up:
A short while only, then I come, she carols – but is only
A fat-lot-of-good mother with a pointless alibi: 'I didn't
Know.' Yet might there still be some part for me
To play upon this lovely earth? Say. Or
Say *No,* earth at my inner ear.

'The eclipse'

Acacias domed by a quick breeze into
shivery plumes, bunched then sinking.
Dusk, crossroads, walker, flats, night.
That rapid wordless halt bewilders me.
Now evening will hold still for years.
Fear has clamped on its stiffened face.
It knows what should have been done.
It understood what it turned away from.

Orphic

I've lived here dead for decades – now you
pitch up gaily among us shades, with your
freshly dead face all lit up, beaming – but
after my long years without you, don't think
it will be easy. It's we dead who should run
whispering at the heels of the living, yet you
you'd put the frighteners on me, ruining
the remains of your looks in bewailing me
not handling your own last days with spirit.
Next you'll expect me to take you around
introducing some starry goners. So mother
do me proud and hold your white head high.
On earth you tried, try once again in Hades.

Percy's Relique;
on the Death of John Hall's Peacock

Earl Percy of Brook Mill, in gown
Of brown with azure trimmings, flown!

Grand and admired fowl, indenturing
John your janitor to toss you copious nuts,

Rare! Raoaark! Rare! You were adornment.
You were Brook Mill. Its visitors were yours.

You Shelley to us duller poets, Percy. Flare!
Go, glittering! Your fan recalls you from her desk

Lamenting, where our London peafowls droop
And sigh for iridescent Percy and his shrieks.

An awkward lyric

It sits with itself in its arms. Out of
the depth of its shame it starts singing
a hymn of pure shame, surging in the throat.
To hold a true note could be everything.
Getting the hang of itself would undo it.

Never to disinter the pink companion

Never to disinter the pink companion. Wintry. So isn't everyone drawn to human warmth, if only by animal curiosity? Seems not. Then how pleasantly to give back his enigma of wordless absence to its real owner, like a jacket he'd not realised he'd left behind? Worse, he had: 'Thanks a lot for another trip to the charity shop.' To confess my bafflement with grace. So, tolerant Grace, though I've needed to call for you so often, please don't ignore my knocks but uncoil from your couch and ease out of your door, smiling, to me mulish with a little scar literature, it is a very late form of love.

CANADIAN
SHORTLIST

JORDAN ABEL

Injun

Jordan Abel's collection *Injun* evacuates the subtexts of possession, territory, and erasure. Lyric, yes: 'that   part of sparkling / kn ife love that // hates   the trouble of rope / and the   letters / of tow   ns." Testimony of another kind, too: "all misdeeds at the milk   house / all heap shoots by the sagebrush // all the grub   is somewhere / down in the hungry bellies [. . .]." The fog of tedious over-dramatization clears and the open skies of discourse can be discerned. What does it mean to arrange hate to look like verse? What becomes of the ugly and meaningless? Words are restored to their constituent elements as coun-termovements in Abel's hands, just as they are divested of their capacity for productive violence. The golden unity of language and its silvered overcoding erode, bringing to bear the "heard snatches of comment / going up from the river bank." To pixelize is to mobilize, not to disappear.

a)

he played injun in gods country
where boys proved themselves clean

dumb beasts who could cut fire
out of the whitest[1] sand

he played english across the trail
where girls turned plum wild

garlic and strained words
through the window of night

he spoke through numb lips and
breathed frontier[2]

b)

he heard snatches of comment
going up from the river bank

all them injuns is people first
and *besides for this buckskin*

why we even shoot at them
and *seems like a sign of warm*

dead as a horse friendship
and *time to pedal their eyes*

to lean out and say the truth[3]
all you injuns is just white keys

c)

some fearful heap
some crooked swell

bent towards him
and produced a pair

of nickel-plated pullers
a bull winder of

dirty tenderness[4]
that stiffened into

that low-brow ice
that dead injun game

h)

who slanted[10] their memories
on   the backs of lids

who breathed on granite
without the   straight

who   squared their mines
bearing down on grubstake

who talked the signs
through   call and country

who   kept their dreams
in some scrape   town

i)

pockets filled   with knives
the camp fixed to a clasp

   a two-year-old   one eye
closed and sideways glancing

a licked   glass of jelly
bordering[11] an artful   territory[12]

a partial injun tongue
steady in an old mans fingers

blankets   over tender feet

j)

if prayers were   tolerable
        if money[13] shook like rattlers

trouble now   up   in the air
concerns over missing   knives

        after all *if a fella dont shoot*
no one man   can change him

because *a man can be anybody*
        except   little

even snakes are more vital
even bandages   wash away

k)

just the warpath[14]
just the all time disgust

  ringing rescue
  acts for the boys and
  injuns for the nights

all misdeeds at the milk house
all heap shoots by the sagebrush

  all the grub is somewhere
  down in the hungry bellies

of drunks all the dog cries
  are announced
  at the back door

himself clean strain that night, the **whitest** little Injun on the reservati
s along the Missouri River had the **whitest** lot of officers that it was eve
it is spirit. He smiled, showing the **whitest** and evenest teeth. Such ext
Jerry wants to talk to you. He's the **whitest** of the lot, if you can call tha
not observe that his teeth are the **whitest**, evenest." "They make them
oked from face to face. "You're the **whitest** bunch—I'd like to know—
n't much just to look at, but he's the **whitest** man I ever knew. You wait
ll you see Blanco Sol! Bar one, the **whitest**, biggest, strongest, fastest, g
el rolls, pure, clean, and sweet, the **whitest** and finest in the world! Am
d her, anyway. Monty Price was the **whitest** man I ever knew. There's N
ne. Al Auchincloss always was the **whitest** an' squarest man in this she
An' Coles swore thet Wade was the **whitest** man he ever knew. Heart o
lousy and be half decent. He's the **whitest** man I ever knew. "Now list
te of Colorado you're known as the **whitest** of the white. Your name's a
with startlin' truth. Wade was the **whitest** man I ever knew. He had a

ge. San Antonio at this time was a **frontier** village, with a mixed popu

s and asked none in return. In this **frontier** village at a late hour one ni

passing glance. Interesting as this **frontier** life was to the young man,

the work before them. There was a **frontier** on the south and west of ov

edit due for guarding this western **frontier** against the Indians and ma

ne soil, as a boy the guardian of the **frontier** was expert in the use of fire

nds. In the use of that arbiter of the **frontier**, the six-shooter, they were

near to hear him. His years on the **frontier** were rich in experience, th

ave it to the stronger republic. This **frontier** on the south has undergon

unties in Texas while it was yet the **frontier**, and by industry and econo

n the early days usually graced the **frontier** towns with their presence.

inner said that he had been on the **frontier** some little time, and that t

at the Ford was quite a pretentious **frontier** village of the squatter type

lassify him at a passing glance as a **frontier** gambler. As we turned awa

ern trail. On morning opposite that **frontier** village, Parent and I took t

another trail drover. Sutton was a **frontier** advocate, alike popular wi

d had grown into manhood on the **frontier**. Sponsilier was likewise ple

ad herd. It was a unique posse. Old **frontier**smen, with patriarchal bear

3)

id that there was a great amount of **truth** mingled with the humor. Son

d spectacle before him. Then as the **truth** gradually dawned upon him,

er children to fear God and tell the **truth**. My vigil was trying to one of

packs. That once, at least, I told the **truth**. Every mother's son of them

and they never shook me from the **truth** of it. I soon learned that robb

on your head if you're telling us the **truth**, only do as you're told, for we

ion to go: 'Son, if you've told us the **truth**, don't look back when you rid

gave him free license to call it. The **truth** is, I didn't pay any more atten

. Half the teamsters, good, honest, **truth**ful men as ever popped a whip

now everything. I must tell her the **truth**, and I'd hate to tell her we bu

This ability to protect himself; and **truth** compels me to say that the ou

k, and by mining a little where his **land** was untillable, and farming a l
an caught him." "Bet you couldn't **land** him," chuckled Baumberger, b
op—and that there makes mineral **land** of it, and as such, open to entr
ut of covering up valuable mineral **land** on purpose. And he says the la
y innocent, too. It was: "Expect to **land** big one to-night. Plenty of sma
ns. He's a high authority—General **Land** Office Commissioner, if you p
all mineral deposits discovered on **land** after United States Patent then
pretty worried, chicken, over that **land** business." Miss Georgie offere
hanged my mind, and thought I'd **land** on you and trust to the lessons
mes to see Miss Georgie about this **land** business. She's wise to a lot of l
through a little gateway which the **land** left open by chance and was hi
al. Mile upon mile, they chose the **land** that pleased them best; and by
d at the peace and the plenty in the **land** which lay around the bay. Cha
ion which made for trouble in that **land** where the primal instincts lay

HOA NGUYEN

Violet Energy Ingots

Hoa Nguyen's poems tread delicately but firmly between the linear demands of narrative and syntax on the one hand and between registers of speech and forms of address on the other. There are spaces for breath, and asides hovering in parentheses. There are also the slippages in language, in the slide from, say, "staring" through "starving" and "starring" to "scarring." Everything is at once tangential yet surprisingly direct. This is where the pleasure and depth reside: in the off balancing of the language and its pure, uncalculated tone. What are the poems about? Many things, often simple and direct, like food, or sex, or rivers, or sickness. The poems are packed with fine precisions and particulars. But there is politics, too, sometimes startlingly straight, as in the poem about Andrew Jackson, or sharp-edged, as in "Screaming." *Violet Energy Ingots* is a fully mature work in that it is confident of both its voice and its readers' alertness. It makes its own space. It demands it and holds it.

Autumn 2012 Poem

Call capable
     a lemony
light & fragile

Time like a ball and elastic

so I can stop burning the pots

wondering yes   electric stove

She is her   but I don't re-
member   remember
the ashes I obsess   She said

I was obsessed with
(not wanting to work with
ashes)

    Mandible dream
   says the street
& ash work

Haunted Sonnet

Haunt lonely and find when you lose your shadow
secretive house centipede on the old window

You pronounce *Erinyes* as "Air-n-ease"
Alecto: the angry   *Megaera*: the grudging

Tisiphone: the avenger (voice of revenge)
"Women guardians of the natural order"

Think of the morning dream with ghosts
Why draw the widow's card and wear the gorgeous

Queen of Swords crown   Your job is
to rescue the not-dead woman before she enters

the incinerating garbage chute   wrangle silver
raccoon power   Forever a fought doll

She said, "What do you know about Vietnam?"
Violet energy ingots   Tenuous knowing moment

January

January long light
Janus   I see you
God of locks and doorways

two-faced looking in Capricorn
Capricious like the snowy owl
        irruption

We fear heavy body collisions

January   time of doors
time looking back on itself
        God of gates

        spelt and salt

They say when you
walk through a door

you can forget what
    you came for

Machiavelli Notes

Machiavelli conversant
in Italian and Latin (not
Greek)
          never had to have
"official income"

Middle height   black-haired
with a rather small head
reports of thin closed lips

                    He sought after
much— Not really a life of leisure
          but of misfortune—

Took wrong side   was tortured
Proud to have passed the ordeal

Bored with the hicks on his farm

He gave himself readily
to "transient amours"

(A secret hero of mine)

                    Scorpio

First Flowers

Wasps out of the birdhouse
for spring   my boys shook
    out the dead wasps

New fly west
New fly west

for spring? To sip it?
Little gatherings of birds

Why does this feel like weeping?
    (snowdrops)

My friends   we love

It is two kinds of lost
that I'm lost in

After the Murder Ballad

Bring some other fine things
hard full life   atoms springing

No money   No fine things

Flatteringly   we are the cave
      It will be OK in disgrace

She jumped   Came to the river
deep water   Thou restless ungathered

orphan   Tell me your mind
to mend   to drown you in despair

      Let me sing gone
If I can live kicked & choked

Turned around in deep water

Torn

Maybe the striped dress is named "Torn"
because of the angled stripes that don't match
up   Deep V-neck opening and a color called
"blue combo"

I lied to the white observers
in the dream when I said   "Someone
like me"   and I meant in my embodied
difference
          but instead made up a different
reason for the statement and applied gritty
cleaning scrub to my face

To be original is to arise
from a novel organ?

Born at dawn from a severed
circumstance

"Sorry   I won't apologize"

SANDRA RIDLEY

Silvija

The poems in Sandra Ridley's book are potent and beguiling. Words are given the space they need to root and branch. This pace of them engages with the unarticulated, the hidden, the unbearable, as readers encounter five elegies that allude to and invoke trauma, shame, and a profound sense of loss. Given the themes at work in this collection, silence is an essential part of the reading. Ridley conducts and curates that space as liminal. Here's where we understand the scope of the work and concede to bearing witness. Here's where we understand that we will be haunted. And from that silence, the words that emerge have been given the time they need to properly cure and to season in the poem's atmosphere. They reach, as words do, singular and fluent. Ridley's language is persuasive and ripe. "[N]arrow your eyes to the now," the poem requests. Here is "a shame unleashed by plain talk." Beneath these elegies, there is a current, a reprise praising the healer. This current is another root system, an ongoing poem, essential to the collection.

from **Farther / Father**

We brace in the centre / attention / nothing more than this

Far-fetched ruckus / rot-gut fuss / a latched door farmhouse

Taunting / the slap-board remains / rants / lashed feverish

Your day's demands / fraught / cling to the bleak / this filth

In plain sight / *I am a man possessed.*

Beyond two graves / yours and the child's / a sole

Pine fallen from a lack of forest / the sun-downed

Dove-wing unfolds / under night / your closeness

Lies too close.

Unearthing the horizon / uncertain if the sun is low / west

Or rising east / luminous / hourglass tipped to the wheat /

Ghosts / our harvest sheen.

Holder of the dog's bones / night-fallen creek / current home

Borne back / broken / the limp body / still writhing / we will

Never depend upon our eyes.

Submerged / without air / within water / us / small-sacked

In the last hour / the equinox / relinquished / moonward

Out of my sight / a wife's tale / we find you not as we want

You / still where you are / dead on the floor / facing down

The long shadow / incalculable / we await the whimper

Eyes lowering / descent of the casket / no axis spinning /

Stars dying / *no* / they are already gone.

from **Clasp**

Sleep is for the weak.

I collected the reasons against it, which were in every body's mouth.
I marked them down, with, I think, some additions. (You may or
may not remember.)

I feign now pleasure—sleep in splendour—notwithstanding
the sadness of the subject.

(Please read the letter.)

A fool could read the signs.

from **Dirge**

We fail to name this right / without the words

For lapsing / lilies / wilted / in the beginning

Wind caught nothing / your leaf unscrawled.

Whatever we've come to collect / we can't find

The undaunted / spectral / *let's put it this way*

Transverse / the waves lengthen ungraspable

Umbral / fear departing as soon as it's spoken

We turned toward your haunting / a sallowed

Rustle / rustle.

Slender   and   tenuous   in   the   eventual

Velvet   quell   /   weak   pulse   /   (no   echo)

Silenced   /   narrow   your   eyes   to   now.

In Praise of the Healer

Wet by the shallows—our willow.

You do not cry because you cannot. I will not cry because you do not.

You give my hands the weight of your body.

Rest in me.

What I mean is this is where I choose to die.

THE POETS

JORDAN ABEL is a Nisga'a writer currently completing his Ph.D. at Simon Fraser University, where he focuses on digital humanities and indigenous poetics. Abel's conceptual writing engages with the representation of indigenous peoples in anthropology and popular culture. His chapbooks have been published by JackPine Press and above/ground press, and his work has appeared in numerous magazines and journals across Canada. He is an editor for *Poetry Is Dead* magazine and a former editor for *PRISM international* and *Geist*. Abel's first book, *The Place of Scraps*, was a finalist for the Gerald Lampert Memorial Award and won the Dorothy Livesay Poetry Prize. Abel's second book, *Un/inhabited*, was published in 2014. CBC Books named Abel one of 12 Young Writers to Watch (2015).

ABDELLATIF LAÂBI, poet, novelist, playwright, translator, and political activist, was born in Fez, Morocco, in 1942. He was the founder of *Souffles*, a left-leaning literary review banned by the Moroccan government in 1972. An outspoken critic of the authoritarian and theocratic regimes of the Maghreb, Laâbi was imprisoned in Morocco for eight years and later exiled to France. Deemed by Amnesty International a prisoner of conscience, Laâbi received the Prix de la liberté and the Prix international de poésie while imprisoned. He went on to receive the Prix Robert Ganzo de poésie in 2008, the Prix Goncourt de la poésie for his *Œuvre complète* in 2009, and the Grand prix de la francophonie from l'Académie française in 2011.

JANE MEAD is the author of four previous collections of poetry, most recently *Money Money Money | Water Water Water* (2014). Her poems appear regularly in journals and anthologies, and she is the recipient of a Guggenheim Foundation Fellowship, a Whiting Writers' Award, and a Lannan Foundation Completion Grant. She teaches at the low-residency M.F.A. program at Drew University and farms in northern California.

Born in the Mekong Delta and raised in the Washington, D.C., area, HOA NGUYEN studied Poetics at New College of California in San Francisco. With the poet Dale Smith, Nguyen founded *Skanky Possum*, a poetry journal and book imprint in Austin, Texas, their home for 14 years. She is the author of several poetry collections, including *Red Juice: Poems 1998–2008* and *As Long As Trees Last*. She lives in Toronto, Ontario, where she teaches poetics privately and at Ryerson University, Bard College, and Miami University.

DONALD NICHOLSON-SMITH is a translator and freelance editor. Born in Manchester, England, and a long-time resident of New York City, Nicholson-Smith has translated, among others, the works of Jean-Patrick Manchette, Thierry Jonquet, Guy Debord, Paco Ignacio Taibo II, Henri Lefebvre, Raoul Vaneigem, Antonin Artaud, Jean Laplanche, and Guillaume Apollinaire. He has also translated many texts dealing with psychology and social criticism. He won the 2015 French-American Foundation Translation Prize for his translation of Manchette's *The Mad and the Bad*.

ALICE OSWALD lives in Devon, England, and is married with three children. Her previous collections include *Dart*, which won the 2002 T. S. Eliot Prize, *Woods etc.* (Geoffrey Faber Memorial Prize), *A Sleepwalk on the Severn* (Hawthornden Prize), *Weeds and Wild Flowers* (Ted Hughes Award), and *Memorial*, which won the 2013

Warwick Prize for Writing. "Dunt," included in *Falling Awake*, was awarded the Forward Prize for Best Single Poem.

Multiple-award-winning poet, instructor, and editor SANDRA RIDLEY is the author of three previous books of poetry: *Fallout* (winner of a 2010 Saskatchewan Book Award and the Alfred G. Bailey Prize); *Post-Apothecary* (finalist for the ReLit and Archibald Lampman awards); and *The Counting House* (finalist for the Archibald Lampman Award and chosen as one of the top five poetry books of 2013 in *Quill & Quire*'s Readers' Poll). In 2015, Ridley was a finalist for the KM Hunter Artist Award for Literature. She lives in Ottawa.

DENISE RILEY is a critically acclaimed writer of both philosophy and poetry. She is currently Professor of the History of Ideas and of Poetry at the University of East Anglia, and has taught and researched widely at many institutions in Europe and America.

THE JUDGES

SUE GOYETTE lives in Halifax and has published five books of poems and a novel. Her latest collection is *The Brief Reincarnation of a Girl* (2015). She's been nominated for several awards, including the 2014 Griffin Poetry Prize, and has won the CBC Literary Prize for Poetry, the Bliss Carman, Pat Lowther, and J. M. Abraham poetry awards, and the 2015 Lieutenant Governor of Nova Scotia Masterworks Arts Award for her collection *Ocean*. Sue currently teaches in the Creative Writing Program at Dalhousie University.

JOAN NAVIYUK KANE is the author of *The Cormorant Hunter's Wife*, *Hyperboreal*, *The Straits*, and *Milk Black Carbon*. Her awards include the Whiting Writers' Award, the Donald Hall Prize in Poetry, the American Book Award, the Alaska Literary Award, and fellowships from the Rasmuson Foundation, the Native Arts and Cultures Foundation, and the School for Advanced Research. Kane graduated from Harvard College, where she was a Harvard National Scholar, and Columbia University's School of the Arts, where she was the recipient of a graduate Writing Fellowship. Inupiaq with family from King Island and Mary's Igloo, she raises her sons in Anchorage, Alaska, and is M.F.A. faculty at the Institute of American Indian Arts in Santa Fe, New Mexico.

GEORGE SZIRTES was born in Budapest in 1948 and came to England as a refugee with his parents and younger brother following the Hungarian Uprising of 1956. He grew up in London and trained as a painter in Leeds and London. He is the author of some 15 books of poetry, roughly the same of translation from Hungarian, and a few miscellaneous other books. His first, *The Slant Door* (1979), was joint winner of the Faber Memorial Prize. In 2004 he won the T. S. Eliot Prize for *Reel*, and was shortlisted for the prize again for *The Burning of the Books* (2009) and for *Bad Machine* (2013). His other prizes include the Cholmondeley Award, and the Bess Hokin Prize in the U.S.A. Bloodaxe Books published his *New and Collected Poems* in 2008. It was listed in *The Independent* as one of the Books of the Year. His translations from Hungarian have won international prizes, including the Best Translated Book Award in the U.S.A. for László Krasznahorkai's *Satantango* (2013), and his latest book for children, *In the Land of the Giants*, won the CLPE Poetry Prize for best collection of poetry for children, also in 2013. He is a Fellow of the Royal Society of Literature in the U.K. and of the Széchenyi Academy of Letters and Arts in Hungary. He is married to painter Clarissa Upchurch and recently retired from teaching at the University of East Anglia.

ACKNOWLEDGEMENTS

The publisher thanks the following for their kind permission to reprint the work contained in this volume:

"The third time my mother fell," "Outside the window the trees," "*How will you spend your courage*," "In my dream my mother comes with me," "My mother's every exhale is," "On the phone, my brother Whit," "Silvia asks whether I ever feel," "Her ashes blow off—," and "In the phone photograph" from *World of Made and Unmade* by Jane Mead are reprinted by permission of Alice James Books.

"Good Morning Sun of My Land," "*from* Skinned Alive," "The Wolves," and a selection from "My Dear Double" from *In Praise of Defeat* by Donald Nicholson-Smith, translated from the French written by Abdellatif Laâbi, are reprinted by permission of Archipelago Books.

"A Short Story of Falling," "Flies," "Cold Streak," "Slowed-Down Blackbird," "Sz," and a selection from "Tithonus" from *Falling Awake* by Alice Oswald are reprinted by permission of Jonathan Cape/W. W. Norton & Company.

A selection from "A Part Song i–v," "The eclipse,'" "Orphic,'" "Percy's Relique; on the Death of John Hall's Peacock," "An awkward lyric," and "Never to disinter the pink companion" from *Say Something Back* by Denise Riley are reprinted by permission of Picador.

THE GRIFFIN POETRY PRIZE
ANTHOLOGY 2017

The best books of poetry published in English internationally and in Canada are honoured each year with the $65,000 Griffin Poetry Prize, one of the world's most prestigious and richest international literary awards. Since 2001 this annual prize has acted as a tremendous spur to interest in and recognition of poetry, focusing worldwide attention on the formidable talent of poets writing in English and works in translation. And each year the editor of *The Griffin Poetry Prize Anthology* gathers the work of the extraordinary poets shortlisted for the awards, and introduces us to some of the finest poems in their collections.

This year, editor and prize juror Sue Goyette's selections from the international shortlist include poems from Jane Mead's *World of Made and Unmade* (Alice James Books), Donaldson Nicholson-Smith's *In Praise of Defeat*, translated from the French written by Abdellatif Laâbi (Archipelago Books), Alice Oswald's *Falling Awake* (Jonathan Cape/W. W. Norton & Company), and Denise Riley's *Say Something Back* (Picador). The selections from the Canadian shortlist include poems from Jordan Abel's *Injun* (Talonbooks), Hoa Nguyen's *Violet Energy Ingots* (Wave Books), and Sandra Ridley's *Silvija* (BookThug).

In choosing the 2017 shortlist, prize jurors Sue Goyette, Joan Naviyuk Kane, and George Szirtes each read 617 books of poetry, from 39 countries, including 23 translations. The jurors also wrote the citations that introduce the seven poets' nominated works. Royalties generated from *The Griffin Poetry Prize Anthology 2017* will be donated to UNESCO's World Poetry Day, which was created to support linguistic diversity through poetic expression and to offer endangered languages the opportunity to be heard in their communities.